A Temporary Silence

poems within the silence

Also by James McGrath from Sunstone Press:

At the Edgelessness of Light, 2005
Speaking With Magpies, 2007
Dreaming Invisible Voices, 2009
Valentines and Forgeries, Mirrors and Dragons, 2011
The Sun is a Wandering Hunter, 2015
A Festival of Birds, 2017
Mixed Greens, 2019

A Temporary Silence

poems within the silence

James McGrath

"It's not just language that we use to write poems. We use silence too.
In fact, we use language to inflect silence so we can hear it better."
—Li-Young Lee, *Breaking the Alabaster Jar*, 2002

SUNSTONE PRESS
SANTA FE

Quotations from various poets and writers are from *Quote Poet Unquote* by Dennis O'Driscoll, Copper Canyon Press, 2009.

Cover photograph: Mountain Province, The Philippines, 1985; black and white ink-wash drawings, 2020, by James McGrath.

Back cover photograph: Daniel Forest, 2020.

Sunstone books may be purchased for educational, business, or sales promotional use.
For information please write: Special Markets Department, Sunstone Press,
P.O. Box 2321, Santa Fe, New Mexico 87504-2321.
Printed on acid-free paper

Library of Congress Cataloging-in-Publication Data

Names: McGrath, James, 1928- author.
Title: A temporary silence : poems within the silence / James McGrath.
Description: Santa Fe, NM : Sunstone Press, [2021] | Summary: "Poems by a
    well-known Southwestern US writer and teacher"-- Provided by publisher.
Identifiers: LCCN 2021035670 | ISBN 9781632933553 (paperback)
Subjects: LCGFT: Poetry.
Classification: LCC PS3613.C497 T46 2021 | DDC 811/.6--dc23

LC record available at https://lccn.loc.gov/2021035670

WWW.SUNSTONEPRESS.COM
SUNSTONE PRESS / POST OFFICE BOX 2321 / SANTA FE, NM 87504-2321 /USA
(505) 988-4418

DEDICATION

I dedicate this gathering to two unrivaled New Mexico poets, Catherine Ferguson and Cynthia West, who shared days, weeks and months of writing via telephone during the temporary silence of the coronavirus period.

POEM
    FOR POET
    CYNTHIA WEST

When I walk the steps
    to your door,
    you share the poem
    you wrote
    when the moon and stars,
    the corn and dahlias
    of you
    broke open the seeds
    you received
    from the mountain.

POEM
    FOR POET
    CATHERINE FERGUSON

When alone,
    I see your hands
    writing with the gold
    of October leaves,
    the feathers of a flicker,
    the ripples of the river,
    the nose of your dog,
    your words falling
    into lines
    remembering rain.

CONTENTS

INTRODUCTION

A Temporary Silence voices that place between what was, what is and what lies ahead. The poems in this collection reflect the thoughts of James McGrath's 92 years of life. He speaks of the "dark waters" before birth and the darkening journey toward the great Hereafter, laced with enchanting moments of child-like wonder and the innocence of a lover's heart. He also dares to boldly depict the heart-wrenching moments of these times we live in: refugees who after a long grueling journey to escape the life-threatening horrors of their own country get caught in the sadistic cruelties of this country. His poetry is at once an eye opener and a healing. Equally poignant are poems such as "Mirage" that open the doors of the exquisite realm of surreal beauty:

"My dreams are the wanderers
*   left in the hands*
*   of a stranger who walks with my shadow."*

One senses in this collection the voice of silence itself—a silence that is spacious; a silence that screams. A silence rich with stories, awaiting the poet to give it words. This silence dictates to him its mysteries and its secrets.

James' life is a poem unto itself. He lives tucked away in the country of the area called La Cieneguilla just on the outer edge of Santa Fe, New Mexico. His home is an old adobe which once was the local stage coach stop. It is befitting that James, himself a world traveler, should live in a stage coach stop where the traffic went in and out.

After what seems like a long bumpy dirt road, the visitor parks their car in the area below the house. The instant you exit the car you sense you have entered a different world, one that is at once ancient and untamed. The steep cliffs on one side are rich in petroglyphs that tell the story of centuries gone by. Everything is ALIVE! Everywhere is a story. Find the pathway to the house taking care not to disturb the giant ant hill right in the middle of the path. Walk on past the large vegetable garden heavy with the crop-of-the-day awaiting harvest. Stop to notice the many bird feeders busy with birds of all colors and sizes. And do be careful not to step on Ralph, the five foot rattlesnake who is enjoying a nap in the sun. You quickly realize that you are a visitor in this world of non-discrimination that welcomes *all* life forms. The Hispanic doors to the house open to the kitchen wafting with good things to eat. The last embers of a glowing fire in the kiva fireplace suggests that cold weather is not far away. James is there to greet you with that twinkle in his opalescent blue eyes. The multi-colored cat named Pumpkin-Spice is somewhere close by and will appear as soon as she feels it's safe to do so.

This is James' home. It is where he lives and sleeps with his Angels of inspiration, as evidenced by the poem, "This Is Where I Welcome You:"

"Here is peace,
   Where my shadow
Takes the shape
   Of who loves me.
This is where I live.
This is where I welcome you."

This collection of poems embraces fantasy, realism, surrealism and memory in the making. The poems are pieces in the puzzle of life that outline the corners and the edges, but leave it up to imagination as to what is yet to come. It ends with an earthy poem in which James and his beloved cats are preparing the soil in the garden for another spring ... in which he has now become an ancestor, just as it should be.

To attempt a portrait of James McGrath is bigger than my arms or imagination can reach. It's clear that he is somehow akin to Native Americans. He has worked with Native people both at the Institute of American Indian Arts in Santa Fe and on the Hopi reservation where he taught art, returning his Native students to the source materials of grinding local stone mixed with glue to use as the color for paintings. It's clear that his roots are Irish, from that ancient land where poetry was born. It's true that in some ways he's as American as apple pie. It's also true that he is a man of the world.

No portrait would be complete without mention of his orchard readings where on balmy spring and summer afternoons friends and poets leave their cars and their worries behind and load their arms with delicious things to eat while walking the short distance step by step on the uneven dirt path to his magical orchard. It is a walk into timelessness. If you look closely at the bows of the trees you will see that they are adorned with wisps of poetry. Poets come from all over to read their work: Rae Taylor from

Canada, and John McGrath all the way from Ireland, as well as outstanding local poets from Santa Fe and the neighboring area. It's a feast of the year's bounty. At the end of a transporting afternoon no one wants to leave.

The world has changed tremendously since 1928 when James McGrath was born in the state of Washington. His father used to take young James deer hunting with him in the woods, but James always preferred communing with the flowers than making a kill. His father taught him to hunt, his mother taught him to make jam from the summer's harvest and preserves from the garden as well as mouth-watering pies and yummy everything. A master at the art of living, James also excels as a fine art painter, world traveler, loving friend, father and grandfather. At 92 he has outlived the young ones.

The technology-driven world of today left James with few choices: either get on board or be left behind. James chose to let technology go on without him. He has no cell phone, no computer, no iPad, no widgets, no nothing. He lives in a technology-free world. He used to type out his poems on an old Sears typewriter that probably would bring quite a price in an antique store, but then it broke so James returned to longhand. In spite of refusing these time-saving devices he's the most creative and prolific person I've ever known. He's unstoppable! This world is a better place for the presence of James McGrath.

It is an honor to be chosen to write the introduction to his latest collection of poetry, *A Temporary Silence*. In this fast-moving world of today James is to be commended for remaining grounded through this temporary silence. His life and his poetry are a timeless wonder as evidenced in his poem, "Wearing the Mask" which he wrote during the COVID-19 pandemic:

"At last,
 We can see the truth
 of one another.
Today,
 The day-of-the-mask,
 our eyes give us the clear path
 to the heart of one another."

—Paulette Frankl, artist and author of
Lust for Justice: The Radical Life and Law of J. Tony Serra and
Marcel & Me: A Memoir of Love, Lust, and Illusion.

PREFACE

---poems within the silence are a written affirmation within the silence and noise of 2019, 2020, 2021, those unpredictable months of the worldwide corona virus threat.

Being surrounded by a barely controlled virus offers the gifts of creative opportunities. These are the years of entering my '90s, receiving a pacemaker, accepting the deaths of two daughters. I began a new orchard of apple, pear, cherry, plum and peach. I relished the gift of being nominated for a Pushcart Prize for my poem, "The Dream of Byron Xol." For a poet-heart, writing is essential. With two generous local poets, we developed a method of writing and sharing on the telephone. Many poems in *A Temporary Silence* are from within that gift of sharing.

As the poet, I believe in the scratching-silence of the pen marking sheets and scraps of paper, relieving the soul-mind of the clutter, the clatter, the listening, the gasping, the energetic silence within.

It is as if the months of the virus uncovered the fragility, the strength of uncertainty in my life and the beliefs, the what-and-the-how bewilderment of the culture I live in.

Is there a word for the silence that dwells within our journey home?

It could be *cloud* or *mirror*.

It could be *moss, bamboo, cerulean blue.*

It might be Greek, *Parakalo.*

It might be Spanish, *Sombra.*

It could be *whale* or *singer.*

For 92 years, I have enlarged, diminished, polished and dulled the silence within.

Silence survives the racket and hush of the world, often wears a mask whether there is a virus or not. The silence within carves lines in my face, lies awake at night when I sleep, speaks the language understood by cats, dogs, apple trees, wild roses, stones.

It is both *pumice* and *basalt.*

I know silence walks alone, beside me.

--James McGrath

WALKING ALONE

"Being everywhere at once
while going nowhere in particular
is what poets do."

—Adam Gopnik,
The New Yorker, 2002

Walking alone is leaving the shadows behind.

Who Do I Ask?

Who do I ask the final question:
     "Where is my grave?"

Once, lately,
     I thought it was my shadow
     who followed me home.
     I asked, "Where is my grave?"

     The answer was an indecipherable hum
     as if they could not decide
     what to tell me.

Later, briefly,
     in yesterday's dream,
     someone in a passing crowd,
     stopped, held out a hand,
     asked for my hand
     to read my palm.
     I asked, "Where is my grave?"

     I am listening.

     Why does the line in my palm
     become so long?

Now, when the cat comes in
     from watching birds,
     she looks at me
     with secrets in her eyes.
     I ask, "Cat, you have listened
     to birds. You have wandered
     my garden and read the lines

of lizards in the dust.
You have wisdom.
Cat, where is my grave?"

Cat looks at me, tail erect.
Cat walks to her chair.
Jumps.
Circles three times.
Lies down.
Curls.
Closes her eyes.

31 August 2020
La Cieneguilla; Santa Fe, New Mexico

via telephone with Catherine Ferguson

Published in *passager*, Winter 2020

POEMS IN THE TEMPORARY SILENCE

No poem is lost in the temporary silence
    of walking alone
    when words are left behind
    among pottery shards and
    tracks of deer in the garden.

These are poems of silence
    when leaves vibrate
    and autumn sunflowers
    leave stars of pollen
    for ants to dust their antennae.

These are poems the bark of trees
    have been waiting for,
    a translator of apples and pears.

These are poems left in the garden
    after the harvest,
    after the earth gives
    its deep sigh to rest
    for another winter.

These are poems artists and poets,
    children and eagles,
    here in the temporary silence
    that is their true voice,
    the voice that sings of rain.

No poem is lost in the silence
    of clouds passing
    or in the flight of doves.

When poets close their eyes,
	the memory of being born
	in the wordless world
	of beginning light,
	is the poem born with
	the memory of a star.

This is when a poet knows
	silence is the poem
	they will always share.

27 August 2020
La Cieneguilla; Santa Fe, New Mexico

WATER AND WAVES

I like the way
        watercolors mix on sheets of water:
        the mixing, the emerging of forms
        to dance with,
        to create music to:
        edges of blue bending into purple
        when caught in the fingers of red.
        Yellows that become orange,
        moustaches, hair wisps of green.

Then the tide comes in,
        covers the trails of sand crabs,
        floats mounds of foam and broken shells
        back into the waves.

It's all about water and waves just now.

Somewhere a forest of pine and aspen
        holds the secret to life here
        in this place, year after year
        of willows and raspberries.

Survival takes a long time in the desert.

Mix the red of Clines Corners
        with the white alkaline of Comanche Gap
        and the sun rises.

Carved birds burst from basalt stones,
        bringing blue eggs to our open hands.

With brushes of rabbit hair and bleached bones
        of wild horses, I paint the portrait
        of the stranger who left a basket
        of prickly pear fruit and juniper berries
        at my door.

Survival takes a long time in the desert.

27 November 2020
La Cieneguilla; Santa Fe, New Mexico

AND WHAT IS THIS I AM DREAMING?

It was the ancestors who dreamed me.

Great Grandfather may be feeding the chickens.

The first chick breathing the shell, peeping,
        emerging in the straw.

Great Grandmother washing the cracked bowls
        they just ate their oatmeal in for breakfast.

Their morning table thoughts warm as
        their chicken feather mattress.

Their dreams, opening their door,
        stepping from the creaking porch,
        down the path to the garden,
        where the eyes of potatoes
        are watering the dry earth.

30 November 2019
La Cieneguilla; Santa Fe, New Mexico

Do We Ask Knotholes To Speak?

There never was a face in the window.

It is not like seeing footprints carving
        the dusty road.

Faces appear in weathered wooden floors,
        on gates, in shadows that rest
        under tables.

Knotholes can be eyes or mouths
        of a stranger.

Faces spring from slices of bread
        and in oil slicks on highways
        in the rain.

Today, I might stand there listening,
        but no mouth in an oil slick
        or in a slice of bread
        has much to say
        as they spoke before
        when I was young.

Do we ask knotholes to speak?

Do we expect faces in water stains
        on our kitchen walls to smile?

Would you walk barefooted
        over a woman grinning
        on your bedroom floor?

Should the old man in the summer cloud
        come again, I would ask him,
        where is he going,
        before he changes into a bear
        and stumbles over the mountain.

3 July 2020
La Cieneguilla; Santa Fe, New Mexico

via telephone with Catherine Ferguson

Naomi

Naomi was the blind girl
      rubbing her hands together,
      pressing her skirt almost thread bare,
      winding her fingers together
      into woven traps for flies
      or bits of newspaper.

Naomi's hands were begging to create
      gifts to the world.

I gave her a ball of clay.

She held as if it was alive.

She felt roundness,
      not egg roundness,
      but an empty roundness.

"There is something inside."

With her thumb and fingers,
      she began a gentle pull-and-push
      of the clay.

Naomi would giggle.

She began to shape
      what she felt inside
      that ball of clay.

She began to giggle with tears.

Naomi was all hands and fingers.

Naomi was clay.

The clay became the shape
     of the first human hand from God.

The clay was Naomi.

10 June 2020
La Cieneguilla; Santa Fe, New Mexico

via telephone with Cynthia West

The Question

I don't count the times
        I asked the question of my paint and brush:
        will you tell the truth?

It was her portrait.

She had the eyes of fire opals.
        There were always sparks
        that caught the air on fire.
        Only tears could put out
        the flames in her eyes.

If I closed her eyes
        with a broken line of black,
        sadness would lie there on her cheeks.

If I left her eyes open,
        she would stare,
        put me in the corner shadows
        with the dust balls.

But that was years ago
        when I could paint innocence
        and loss without tears.

I could write poems
        that stained the collars
        of white shirts.

I could draw a portrait of her
        that crumpled the paper.

I could walk across a room
        to greet her
        with the legs and feet
        of a dragon.

But that was years ago
        when I would not wait
        for apples to ripen.

Now, I only want to keep
        my eyes open
        to see her
        when I sleep.

25 May 2020
La Cieneguilla; Santa Fe, New Mexico

via telephone with Catherine Ferguson

Naming

If I call you willow,
     it is because you walk
     without a shadow.

If I call you Cosmos,
     it is because your face
     has the color and openness
     of an apple blossom.

If I call you Columbine,
     it is because I feel
     your beating heart
     when you drink tea with me
     sitting next to plum blossoms.

My name for you changes from season to season.

In Spring,
     I will call you Sprouting Corn.
     Your arms become ribbons
     of sunlight.

In Summer,
     I will call you Fledgling Towhee.
     Your colors, the shattering
     of a rainbow.

In Autumn,
     I will call you Ripening Pear.
     Your voice, the echo
     of falling feathers
     of early migrating birds.

In Winter,
     I will call you Sky Mirror.
     You will touch my cheek
     with snow flakes
     as if the moon has finger tips
     to wipe the cold tears away.

I have many names for you
     because you hide in my dreams
     whispering, *I love you.*
          I love you.

10 May 2020
La Cieneguilla; Santa Fe, New Mexico

via telephone with Cynthia West

To Keep The Fire Alive

In this time of virus,
    even in Summer,
    keeping the fire alive
    is for the poet;

    red of geraniums,
    smell of smoke,
    sun in the mud puddle,
    standing barefoot on the street corner,
    walking alone.

    Creating the path into Autumn,
    Winter is
    stepping lightly,
    stomping on shadows,
    stuttering,
    fanning the embers into the smallest flames,
    finally, scorching the paper with words
    covered in a mask that forces hands
    into gloves unable to press juice
    from haunted houses.

It takes one match
    to burn a memory
    into ashes.

24 October 2020
La Cieneguilla; Santa Fe, New Mexico

via telephone with Catherine Ferguson

Old Ghosts Do Not Like Loneliness

We do not want
        to remember loneliness
        until we need
        echoes of sadness
        to keep us awake.

Old ghosts are a different thing,
        we welcome them or not.

Those old ghosts
        have a movable shrine
        of their own
        that may be on the pages
        of a book, or in the brief line
        of a song from childhood.

Old ghosts do not like loneliness,
        they prefer laughter.

Old ghosts wait for us to knock
        on any door of the hundreds
        we keep closed. We do not need keys
        or a secret password,
        a memory will do.

Old ghosts have the kindness
        of familiar strangers who remain
        waiting for us just around
        the corner.

Should a lonely old ghost appear
        uninvited, perhaps they are only

asking to be touched by
a kind word, the word we failed
to give them the last time
we met.

Could it be that loneliness is there
        in that last word we left unsaid?

An old ghost might have an answer
        to that question.

When the old ghost comes again
        in that dream or
        pages of the book or
        humming the song of childhood,
        then we can ask,
        "What can I give you
        you do not already have?"

One day, you and I will be old ghosts.
        We must have an answer to
        that same question:
        "What can I give you
        you do not already have?"

19 May 2020
La Cieneguilla; Santa Fe, New Mexico

She Saw The Future Through The Eye Of Her Needle

The quilt.

She sewed when he was in the field
	with plow and seeds.

She sewed when he was in the barn
	with cows and horses.

She sewed when he slept without dinner.

She sewed, pieces of his denim shirts,
	his scent stitched into the seams.

She sewed, pieces of her flower-printed dresses
	from Blue Bird Flour sacks,
	fragments of their children's school clothes.

She sewed in her dreams.

She sewed in her memories
	of the children growing into men
	and women.

She sewed in the sour-milk of summer.

She sewed in the frozen calves of
	the ice-age winter.

She sewed in the acres of drought-dead
	cornfields.

She sewed in the horse struck by lightning.

She sewed the quilt to cover his casket.

She had sewed her body next to his body.

10 August 2018
Galisteo, New Mexico

How To Pray

On the pathway
        to the mountains,
        the feet of pine trees
        have left the stones
        to themselves.

Such respect
        is given to fallen leaves
        by beetles and worms
        who go about their own business.

And those pussy willows
        who come briefly
        before cottonwood buds,
        their pearl sized softness,
        the open eyes of the Mother.

Should we shake hands
        with the rattle shells
        of yucca or the golden
        flower heads of chamisa,
        we might learn
        what a falling feather knows:
        how to fall to the earth
        without a map.

This is how to pray without a word.

11 March 2020
Santa Fe, New Mexico

Rain

The trees in the field
      breathe light
      in the morning,
      their leaves
      whispering stories
      of moonlight
      and strangers wandering
      along the fence line.

There is always
      a stranger wandering
      along the fence line
      avoiding the barbed wire teeth,
      strangers who appear
      to be searching for something lost.

How they ignore the lines of poetry
      etched in the fence posts.

How they forget their footsteps
      will fill with mint after a rain.

How their perspiration on hot days
      have the scent of sage,
      their ears humming with
      songs of grasshoppers.

I was a stranger once like you.

Now I sit among house sparrows
      and July thrashers
      who tell me stories

of strangers like you
wandering along fence lines
leaving their footsteps
in the dust to fill with mint
after a rain.

3 July 2018
Galisteo, New Mexico

A Poet Writes

"All we have to do is to be, but simply,
earnestly, the way the earth simply is."
-Rilke

How did the apple tree know
     I was listening
     when its first blossoms
     said, "Spring?"

How did the river know
     to respect its moist dreams
     of rushing from the mountain
     as I sat with magpies?

What stone echoed
     the cliff's voice
     to stand firm on the path
     into the clouds?

Where did the thrashers learn
     the languages of migrating birds
     to keep me still, my heart beating
     in the morning as the sun rises?

Why did it take so long for me to know
     I was tree and river,
     stone and thrasher,
     when all I wanted to do
     was to dance and sing
     my own songs?

6 May 2019
La Cieneguilla; Santa Fe, New Mexico

Then, I Remember

I might believe
    that now
    is the time
    to slip from view,
    to close the curtains,
    roll up the rugs.

Then, I remember,
    it was 8th grade,
    a party in the basement,
    curtains closed,
    rugs rolled up,
    78s on the turntable,
    — like now —
    the turntable
    slowly turning,
    the last slow dance.

4 September 2019
La Cieneguilla; Santa Fe, New Mexico

Small Things, Like Aging

Small things,
        like aging,
        change the shape of the world.

Countries on the roll-down map
        vanish.

Rocks that trundle down the mountain
        settle into their own shadows.

Feathers of birds left at my door
        become brushes to change the color
        of my eyes nesting what I see
        in my garden, season by season.

Now is the time in my life
        I sit under the trees I cherish
        to catch falling leaves,
        pressing them into the pages
        of my own silent orchard.

The luminous child within who holds
        the hands of my dreams,
        never cries again. His long ago tears
        have softened the clay to form the angel
        who waits for me.

I keep rain water in my tea bowl
        with grains of sand from the desert
        where I left my footprints
        long before I could walk.

Small things I left on the teetertotter
        are to be found wrapped in blue lined
        paper from a spelling lesson as I carve
        my name in the bark of a cherry tree.

Small things,
        like aging,
        change the shape of the world.

I never accept apples anymore.

11 August 2020
La Cieneguilla; Santa Fe, New Mexico

via telephone with Cynthia West

SUBJECT TO EXAMINATION

When does a poet
       choose the road
       of word or dream?

Could a poet
       be born with word
       and dream tattooed
       on their forehead?

When does a poet
       choose the path
       of thorny thickets
       and blossoming birds?

Could it be
       that a poet
       has thorny thickets
       and blossoming birds
       wrapped as swaddling clothes
       about the shadow
       with the first breath?

Could a poet
       stop long enough
       on their tireless walk
       on the mad, luxuriant trail
       of bread crumbs
       long enough to know
       bread crumbs are the food
       for what is wild in all of us?

31 August 2020
La Cieneguilla; Santa Fe, New Mexico

via telephone with Cynthia West

Mirage

How I miss you
        when the invisible roots of you
        lie entangled with tulip bulbs
        and the view of snow falling.

This to say,
        you are the eternal journey
        I have taken
        without a map.

My dreams are the wanderers
        left in the hands
        of a stranger
        who walks with my shadow.

We step from stone to stone,
        from mountain to mountain,
        pausing to decipher
        the spiralling of pine cones
        that guide us the way
        through the forest.

Should we find ourselves
        in a canyon without an exit,
        let us lie down together
        to listen for the hoofbeats
        of ghost-horses. We will
        take their reins
        across the desert
        pausing long enough
        to be danced to exhaustion
        by a lonely, distracted dust devil
        I shall name, *mirage*.

21 August 2020
La Cieneguilla; Santa Fe, New Mexico

via telephone with Catherine Ferguson

Who Will Recognize Us

Now is the time
        to find our way
        back into the stars
        where we came from,
        to emerge with more brilliance,
        more sparkle,
        luminous as the moment
        our eyes first saw light,
        after the dark waters.

Now is the time
        to breathe the dust
        of our beginning
        into the new myth
        we were meant to be
        when we emerged
        crying into the light,
        after the dark waters.

Our day hours of sun and green
        are the clothes
        we may hide in
        to walk alone
        to gather that dust
        into the waiting bowl
        where the seed that we are
        will sprout again.

Who will recognize us?

Who will give us our name?

It is not far
      to gather the dust.
      It is all around us.
      This is why Spring
      comes again and again.
      This is the time
      to put our hearts
      into the hands of who loves us
      as we were received
      in the hand that held us
      when we fell into the light,
      after the dark waters.

And that hand,
      it may have been empty,
      it may have been waiting,
      it may have been indifferent,
      yet we arrived,
      alone,
      into the light,
      after the dark waters.

10 May 2020
La Cieneguilla; Santa Fe, New Mexico

via telephone with Cynthia West

WHERE THERE IS NOISE

> "In a time of violence, the task of poetry
> is in some way to reconcile us to our world
> and to allow us a measure of tenderness
> and grace with which to exist."
>
> —Meena Alexander, *The Kenyon Review*, Winter 2005

The noise around us is the silence screaming our names.

A Temporary Silence
-a poem for you when it is noisy.

To be filled with poetry
      is being in harvest,
      to be warm ashes,
      to be on the branch of falling apples.

To ask, where do I go from here,
      is to admit to being filled
      to the edge of stillness.

This is to open the eyes wider
      to see the pen is not empty of ink,
      the paper has no markings,
      no images, crowding the empty, open,
      white silence.

This is to discover the quiet place
      in the crowd, to hum among the noise
      of discontent and loneliness.

This is to know words of praise
      give light to the darkness.

This is not wavering candle light.

This is light to illuminate the lull,
      the standstill, the interruption
      of harvesting the fire-starter
      life of a poet.

15 September 2020
La Cieneguilla; Santa Fe, New Mexico

via telephone with Cynthia West

The Noise Around Us Is The Silence Screaming Our Names

I used to dream bear.

    I could have dreamed dinosaur when I was six.
      Stegosaurus could have lived in the swamp behind
      the house when the washing machine growled
      on Mondays.

    I could have dreamed long-pants when I was ten.
      Two pockets in back for notes to Dorothy and
      a zipper when the cloakroom smelled of rubber
      galoshes when it rained.

    I could have dreamed flying-kite when I was thirteen.
      Uncle was drafted to go to Okinawa when the movie,
      Bambi, left a hole in the ceiling above my bed.

    I could have dreamed Mozart in high school. The choir
      sang Christmas carols at the train depot when pigeons
      roosted in the stations-of-the-cross in grandmother's
      Holy Rosary Church.

    I could have dreamed sleeping in my pajamas the first day of
      college when the sound of car horns scared cows at the
      railroad crossing.

    I never dreamed a crock-of-gold could be found
      in those adobe ruins, nourished by spiders
      and welcomed by dust devils, when gold could be
      melted at such low temperatures.

    I never dreamed a poem could etch love across four
      knuckles of my right hand when heels of my feet
      had been rubbed raw from too much dancing.

    I never left home when snow fell long enough to put
      arms on a snowman.

1 July 2020
La Cieneguilla; Santa Fe, New Mexico

Cages

When images behind your eyes
    are the wounds that will not heal
    just now, remember.

This is the time to dream;
    the time for the body, the heart,
    to listen for birds leaving seeds
    at your door; the time for the daisies
    in the morning to be on your pillow
    so you may pull petal after petal;
    who loves me,
    who loves me not,
    who loves me?
    Daisies never lie.

When the gumdrops you dropped
    along the path are eaten,
    consider the thieving mice
    have taken their journey
    to the mountain where summer
    strawberries are about to ripen.

When you feel the night is too short
    for a dream to include you
    in the crowd at the fountain,
    consider washing your face
    in the tears of the children
    in cages at the border.

Crayons and Mickey Mouse stories
    are not enough to spread
    light and blankets
    on the floors of cages.

A mother can never leave a piece
    of her dress large enough
    to hold all the tears;
    a father can never leave enough
    scent of his moisture to hide

the smell of tuna fish and
orange jello.

Salty tears can not rust iron bars
    on cages quick enough for an escape.

Tigers and bears in zoos
    will tell you this
    when they dream
    and stars listen.

31 July 2020
La Cieneguilla; Santa Fe, New Mexico

via telephone with Catherine Ferguson

Drawing Pictures

In 1940,

in Berlin,

grandfather took my mother by the hand

to market for bread.

SS men grabbed grandfather.

He whispered to mother,

"Run. Hide in the potato sacks.

Do not go home."

Mother never saw her father again.

In 2018,

in Trenton,

father took me by the hand

to walk me to school.

ICE men grabbed father.

He whispered to me,

"Run across the street into the church.

Do not go home."

Today,

I sit with other boys and girls

in the church basement.

We draw pictures of our fathers and mothers.

31 January 2018
La Cieneguilla; Santa Fe, New Mexico

Nominated for a Pushcart Prize by *kerf*,
College of the Redwoods;
Crescent City, California, 2020

This Is What I Could Tell You

I could tell you
        who I am
        if you would listen,
        and be still,
        while I poured my wine
        into your crystal sieve.

I am feeding the feral cat
        who comes before the birds arrive.

You see,
        I think of myself
        as a feral cat.

I want to be at your door
        before the sun rises.

I want to feel the sun
        run down my spine,
        to steal the shadow
        that fills my footsteps.

If I told you
        I married a fox
        when I was twelve,
        would you believe me?

If I told you
        my daughter
        was a butterfly,
        would you believe me?

I am older now.

I have a very long story to tell
        because it has no ending.

I can only tell you,
        the fox I married
        and I have enlarged our den
        to welcome you for the weekend.

My daughter has changed
        her butterfly clothes
        for the wings of an angel.

15 January 2020
Galisteo, New Mexico

The Dream of Byron Xol

Gossip tells me
    I am one of nine
    of 4000 kids
    without father or mother
    who will meet my father
    from Guatemala
    this week
    in Los Angeles, California
    —the Angels—
    sounds like a place
    I belong with my father.

I will leave 3991
    brothers and sisters
    in cages
    scattered across America
    —land of the free and the brave—
    across California, Arizona,
    New Mexico, Texas
    and somewhere called Pennsylvania.

My father
    has a black moustache,
    a big hat, old black shoes
    and a blue shirt.

Will he know me
    after almost two years?
    I am skinny now
    and have bad teeth.

24 January 2020
La Cieneguilla; Santa Fe, New Mexico

A Third Prize winner in the 27th Annual Artists Embassy International's
Dancing Poetry Festival Contest; www.dancingpoetry.com

The Hitchhiker

The old, unprotected man
        on the corner of St. Francis
        and Cordova

—as safe as he can afford to be—

        is vigilant,
        his backpack
        holding yesterday's crackers,
        dog biscuits, a pair of dirty socks
        and the plaid shirt torn
        by the high school gang
        last Saturday;
        the gang that chased and stoned
        his dog until it was lost
        on Cerrillos Road near the deaf school.

That vigilant man and his dog
        are out-of-place in this polluted world,
        like the stones on the hillside
        holding back erosion, but
        seen as being available
        for the rock crusher.

Beyond St. Francis and Cordova,
        beyond Cerrillos Road,
        the vigilant man, a lost dog,
        is the hitchhiking virus
        waiting at a million street corners
        for vigilant, old men, dogs and you

—as safe as elders, dogs and you can afford to be—

Churches on Easter morning
        will hand out chocolate crosses
        to believers,
        part of the president's six trillion
        corona-virus-aid-package.

Old men, dogs, and you may have
        to stand in line

—as safe as they and you can afford to be.

26 March 2020
La Cieneguilla; Santa Fe, New Mexico

Predestination

Where was I before I was here?

On the dusty pathways
    in Sana'a
    between carved buildings,
    white *galabayyas* vanishing
    around the corner of the *souk*,
    gray donkeys fading
    into mud and stone walls.

The scent of boiling fenugreek.

It is Thursday.

Fuad and Nabil are bringing
    qat this afternoon.

Uncle is up in the *muffrage*
    with his *oud*,
    says, "There has not been a song
    worth singing since 700."

"When do we stop grieving, Uncle?"

"Insha' Allah, ebn al' akh."

       Sana'a: capital of Yemen
       galabayya: a long, loose robe
       souk: a market
       muffrage: a room with cushion, water pipe where men social-
       ize

qat: an intoxicant herb
oud: a lute-like instrument
Insha' Allah: if God wills
ebn al' akh: nephew

8 February 2021
La Cieneguilla; Santa Fe, New Mexico

CALL OUT THE ELDERS

Call out the elder.

Call out the elder,
        she isn't sleeping,
        she is tending the fires,
        she is creating new recipes
        for our kindergarten.

Call out the elder.

Call out the elder,
        he isn't sleeping,
        he is tending the waters,
        he is propagating the desert lands
        for the Garden.

Call out the elders.

Call out the elders.

Look in the fragments of the mirror
        hidden in the stones. Clean them
        to a polish to reflect the eyes
        of the ancestors who have wept
        their last tears.

Call out the elders.

Call out the elders.

Skip through the cemeteries

cleaning the names on the stones
so they will remind us
who they are and what they
left behind in our shopping carts.

Call out the elders.

Call out the elders.

Add a thousand days, a thousand weeks,
    a thousand months, years to your age.
    Walk into the mall, the plaza,
    the circus. Some child will recognize
    you: *"There's an old lady!"*
      "There's an old man!"

Give that child your tootsie roll.
    Paste a gold star on their forehead.

Then, then, go stand on a street corner
    with cars streaming past,
    with your sign:
      "I am an elder!"
      "I am an elder!"

27 April 2020
La Cieneguilla; Santa Fe, New Mexico

WEARING THE MASK

"The making of poems is mysteriously tied up
with not-knowing, with willing ignorance
and an openness to mutation."

—Tony Hoagland, *The American Poetry Review*, July-August, 2003

Wearing the mask is seeing in the darkness.

Wearing The Mask

At last,
 we can see the truth
 of one another.

Today,
 the day-of-the-mask,
 our eyes give us the clear path
 to the heart of one another.

This does not mean to stare
 unblinking.

Whale watching people
 speak of the light
 coming from the eyes of a whale
 penetrating, offering images
 of peace and becoming fluid
 as the water.

Some Pueblo Indian hunters
 sing of the light
 connecting them to the deer
 they hunt, the connection
 of giving and receiving.

As we place our mask
 over our nose and mouth,
 the string around our ears,
 it is the eyes
 that will give and receive,
 giving what we are holding
 from the sky, the earth,

the memories of what we see
in the light of our dreams;
receiving what comes
into the fertile dirt
of our garden to sprout
the seeds we plant
each day of our lives
for the upcoming harvest.

Just now,
I am thankful for the mask
I wear to greet you,
you greeting me.

Perhaps we shall see one another
again before the moon sets
and we fall asleep again.

14 July 2020
La Cieneguilla; Santa Fe, New Mexico

via telephone with Cynthia West

I Considered Voting

I considered voting.
    I stepped under the cottonwood tree on the corner
    to be caressed by falling leaves.

I considered standing in line
    in my mask,
    in my state of full moon,
    in my state of migrating robins.

I considered the smile, the questions
    of the volunteer who asks,
    "Your name,
    your address,
    your undetermined heart beat?
    Did you vote before?"

I considered answering:
    "I am Jupiter. The shadow of a star.
    My address is the apple tree
    in the orchard at 83 Via de los Romero."

    "Yes. I vote every morning.
    I count the tracks of deer in my garden."

I considered using the black pen filling in
    those oblong shapes to darken my eyes
    to look like the woman killed
    on the street corner in Memphis.

I considered folding the election documents
    into paper cranes
    to toss around the election room.

*"Yes. I am here to vote.
     I am joining the deer in the line
     just behind me."*

8 November 2020
La Cieneguilla; Santa Fe, New Mexico

LOSS OF BREATH: A LOVE POEM

My whispering to you
        is arranging flowers
        in your hair,
        one single breath
        holding falling leaves
        between apple branches
        and tomorrow's teeth.

This is where
        we danced
        loved by bees
        gathering honey
        for winter hours.

My silence with you
        is the mountain
        I climb
        when the moon fails
        to appear in your eyes.

One single breath
        is steaming the window
        in my heart
        where I wrote
        I love you
        with my glass fingertips.

This is where
        we left one another:
        you, following the shadow
        of geese flying South;
        me, staying behind

carving your name
in the bark of the night.

We never
took the stones
from our mouths.

1 December 2019
La Cieneguilla; Santa Fe, New Mexico

This Time

Could it be
        this time,
        —this virus-time—
        is a childhood time for the artist,
        the poet we have kept alive
        waiting for the truth?

Those are not lies
        we kept close to pen and paper.

We just did not have the words then.

Now is the time
        —a virus-time—
        a time to put on a mask,
        to breathe from the heart.

Few listen to us.

They listen to their own heart beats,
        feel their own heat,
        taste their own blood.

The mesa is free to jump from.

The desert is open for running naked.

We can still skip rope
        and play hopscotch with bottle caps.

If we do not see the moon tonight
        before we sleep,

it is only because
we are looking somewhere else.

If our hands are cold in our dreams,
    it is only because
    we choose to sleep alone.

If we misspell words in our poems,
    it is only because
    we write so fast
    thinking there
    is so little time left.

No leaves are falling in the orchard.

25 May 2020
La Cieneguilla; Santa Fe, New Mexico

via telephone with Catherine Ferguson

WE ARE LOVED IN OUR MEMORIES

We are loved in our memories
        that stack one upon another
        in the darkness
        of the book without a cover.

Page after page
        of hopscotch
        and roller skates,
        brownies and butterscotch,
        haircuts and tears.

Chapter after chapter
        of butter scotch squares,
        of holding hands,
        kisses on the street corner,
        park benches.

Volume after volume
        of poems
        that blink
        and fly off the pages
        into the world of silence
        where they join
        winter clouds,
        images
        that change
        and color our dreams
        of how it was
        when we knew who loved us.

15 November 2019
Galisteo, New Mexico

The Right Moment To Fly Away

Can you name
        where you were before
        you were here?

This may be your birth place or
        where the bees left honey
        on your pillow.

No one should ask such questions
        of angels.

These are the questions
        limbs ask when they fall
        on a quiet day
        breaking the heart
        of a tree full of fruit.

A 4-leaf clover
        might give two
        of their 4-leaf answers
        before the moon rises.

There is a dog barking somewhere
        in the valley where fields of
        alfalfa are fenced in
        against coyotes.

This may be the place
        where gophers are safe,
        where raccoons can steal
        eggs of blue jays.

There is an opening in the clouds
        over the Sangre de Cristos
        where eagles fly.

This is the space
        where our shadows
        can leave us behind
        in the tops of pine trees.

When I have left my last shadow
        on the tallest pine branch,
        I will know the right moment to fly away.

26 June 2020
La Cieneguilla; Santa Fe, New Mexico

via telephone with Cynthia West

Time of the Virus

The dead have outnumbered my neighborhood.

Sister of a friend in New Jersey, lost,
        alone, a head-stone, her inviolate new name.

Now the dead sit behind the TV,
        watch through the blackened-window eye,
        stare. They see you and they see me.

No chance to keep their arms around
        each other's shoulders.

They felt nothing but fear,
        if fear is nothing.

Little sensations now. Boredom, loneliness,
        turned to impatience, barely breathing.

A red spot, at the last gasp of breath.

What number is stamped on the forehead?

Even a polaroid will not show the truth.

I had no chance to talk to them through
        the IV drip of tears.

I only remember touching their hands
        as if I was holding my own open,
        outstretched hand.

Any poet will keep the story short.

27 July 2020
La Cieneguilla; Santa Fe, New Mexico

WEARING THE MASK IS SEEING IN THE DARKNESS

I walked the beach of a familiar island where seals left
        their skins on rocks with barnacles to swim naked
        with swirling flags of kelp.

        I stood still at the edge of a dead volcano expecting
            lichens to bloom yellow and orange painting a mask
            across my face.

        I waited for a whale to swallow the man who took my
            childhood but his breath had the smell of garlic.

        I sat in the park on the iron bench with the cast metal
            cherubs listening to their evening vespers
            in Latin expecting candles to burst into flames
            at the parking meters.

        I gathered chestnuts in the forest where Hansel and
            Gretel left candy wrappers for refugee children
            to find their way home before dark.

        I hid under a blanket of pine needles waiting for
            mushrooms and mint to put out the fires before
            the flames reached the mailbox.

        I left a final note in the nest of a robin with
            three blue eggs thinking the sadness of saying
            good-bye would be translated into Greek.

            I walked between the ages of ten and twenty as if
            the world had not begun, and if it rained,
            I could plant the seeds left behind by my father.

        I opened the jar of peaches left in the back-seat
            of the VW bus on a Sunday Morning in September,
            thinking it was my birthday. Yellow jackets
            flew out blinding me.

I write in the dark now.

Wearing the mask is seeing in the darkness.

19 September 2020
La Cieneguilla; Santa Fe, New Mexico

via telephone with Catherine Ferguson

With The Watery Eyes of a Whale

In this time-of-the-mask,
        it is the eyes
        that is the face:
        no nose,
        no mouth,
        neither cheeks nor chin.

It is the eyes that is the face.

This is the time
        when the eyes are all we have
        to interpret the silence around us:
        the color of fear,
        the sound of pain,
        the taste of sorrow and loss.

If we give away all the blue
        or brown of our eyes to strangers,
        what we have left
        may be blindness
        to the moon rising
        over the mountain.

In this time-of-the-mask,
        it is the color of the sunrise,
        it is the sound of the morning birds,
        it is the taste of fresh air
        and the breath of the beloved
        that opens the eyes
        to what is beautiful
        in the eyes of the stranger
        who walks but a few feet away.

I am marking this time-of-the-mask
        on my map toward home
        with the watery eyes of a whale.

29 December 2020
La Cieneguilla; Santa Fe, New Mexico

via telephone with Cynthia West

LIVING ANOTHER YEAR

This is the year
    the wild plums did not fruit
    and the milkweed did not send
    their yearly parachutes across the road.

This is an unruffled year
    among horsetails and willows.

Yet the road-dust still maps the deer
    coming into the garden
    and the cows in Tafoya's field
    remain begging at the fence.

Behind the mountain, the rainbow
    waits for the rain.

Clouds visibly become tired
    changing their shapes
    over-and-over even as winds
    tear them apart pulling rain clouds
    from thirsting desert gardens.

I think of the late summer days
    before school began,
    boys and girls waiting,
    changing from Tarzans and Janes
    into potential teacher's pets
    learning the names of patriotic heroes
    and the names of dogs that barked
    behind gates just before
    we got to the school yard.

I like waiting for a rain
        and thunder storm
        when the sun is shining,
        just before you remove your mask,

22 August 2020
La Cieneguilla; Santa Fe, New Mexico

via telephone with Catherine Ferguson

FINDING HOME

"Poetry, perhaps more than any other literary form, expresses the desire and need to be at home in the universe; to belong."

—G.J. Finch, *Critical Surveys 3, no. 1*

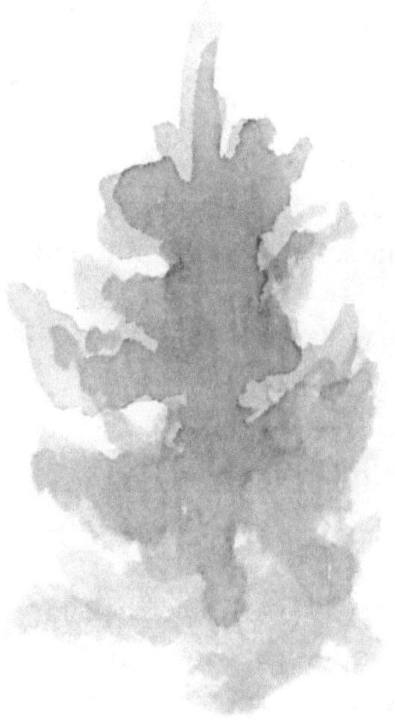

Finding home is finding love on the path we walk together.

The Way Home

There is a well-worn, creased,
        sweat-stained map we carry
        in our silence.

X marking the place, the people,
        the thing that changed
        our life.

We may polish the gold
        of who loved us,
        tarnished from neglect,
        so they outshine the new moon.

We may wipe the dust
        from the place we hid
        our dreams, muzzling
        the scarecrow of childhood.

We may replace the street sign
        to the market where the farmer
        of watercress sprinkled
        rain water on our heads,
        baptizing us, Nesting Bird.

The map remains in the pockets
        of our open hands for us
        to read when the darkness
        is too dark, when we ask
        for the light from the eyes
        of our beloved to see,
        and it is given to us.

The map we carry in silence
    has no North, no South,
    no East, no West.

The map we carry in silence
    is the way home.

11 March 2020
Santa Fe, New Mexico

JESS

Jess has been home now almost two years.

He doesn't laugh very much,
      has a throat-locking, gargle sound;
      says it was the gas.

He doesn't blink his eyes
      when the sun makes the rest of us squint;
      says it was the search lights.

He doesn't comb his hair,
      even when he took Nora to dinner;
      says it's the lice.

He keeps the window over his bed open,
      even in January;
      says he can escape his nightmares.

He made an appointment to change his name
      to Adam;
      says it gives him a fresh start.

He went to the animal shelter
      the first thing when he got back;
      says cats do not give orders.

He washes his clothes all day
      on Saturdays;
      says real soldiers do that.

He pays cash for everything he buys;
      says he earned every cent
      of his disability check.

He can't cut his own fingernails,
        showed me scars on his back;
        says knives and scissors give him the shakes.

He never eats chicken,
        salutes crows and magpies;
        says feathered things are angels.

He built a tree house in the orchard,
        used old jeans and shirts from Goodwill;
        says the tent he carried with him has holes.

He spray-painted the names <u>ROBERT</u>, <u>KEN</u>,
        <u>PHIL</u>, <u>EDDIE</u>, <u>CARLOS</u>, <u>CHIEF</u>, <u>BUD</u>, <u>PETE</u>,
        <u>MAC</u>, <u>JIMMY</u> on the garage walls.

He visits the cows in Tafoya's field,
        leans over the fence, touches noses;
        says they are quiet like Fuad's cow.

He takes his mother and me to the cemetery
        every Sunday.
        We put flowers on his grave.

17 January 2021
La Cieneguilla; Santa Fe, New Mexico

This May Be The Time

So we sit in the afternoon,
      see the sky blue begin to crimson,
      feel the wind losing its heavy voice,
      watch the locust leaves tremble
      in a nervous dance that darkness brings
      to the land after a full day of sun.

This is to begin to quiet,
      to put anxious moments aside,
      to let the heart-shaped petals
      of our wounds join the dust balls
      in the corner of our dreams.

This may be the time to return
      to childhood, to kneel at the
      bedside, close our eyes,
      bless our beloveds,
      ask for the love of the world
      that is swirling, spiraling
      around the men and women
      on the street corners
      for us to remember
      as sister and brother.

These are the times to peacefully
      whoop and holler as bees gather honey
      for winter and fruit in the orchard
      consider ripening because they always have.

31 July 2020
La Cieneguilla; Santa Fe, New Mexico

via telephone with Catherine Ferguson

WHEN I LEAVE

"—there is a likeness between dying and being somewhere that isn't here."
—Conor Cleary, "The American Wake," *Still in the Dreaming:* poems
from Kerry 2017-2018.

When I leave,
    I will leave behind
    a narrow dirt road for you
    to match your footsteps
    with the ribbon-poem of the rattlesnake
    in the dust,
    and the minute etching
    of the feet of mice
    that disappear into the hole
    that was not there yesterday.

As I step over the shadows
    of fence posts lying
    in the road dust,
    there will be splinters
    from when I was told
    not to pick the apples
    before they ripened.

It was long ago.
    I stopped somewhere
    that isn't here.
    I saw my reflection
    in a store window
    where there were roller skates,
    red wagons,
    an orange tricycle
    and a blue-black bicycle
    for older boys:

mechanical things
for unnamed adventures
at the end of the road
that will be left behind
when I leave.

26 December 2018
La Cieneguilla; Santa Fe, New Mexico

Where The Poem Lives

The poem is everywhere.

It hides for a moment only,
        waiting for us to tumble
        out of the shadows.

The thorns in the poem
        catch at our sleeves,
        pull threads
        from our winter coats,
        unraveling our dreams.

At night,
        when our pillows
        hold the moon to our ears,
        we hear stars falling,
        bruising our hearts.

In the morning,
        the light opens our veins
        for words in our poems
        only birds repeat.

We may step
        out of doors,
        breathe the scent
        of passing clouds.

We may write
        our names
        on the stones
        by our doorway,

knowing small bugs
live there.

It is that place
        in our house
        where poems live,
        where we have welcomed
        one another,
        given our poems to strangers
        who knocked on our doors,
        given our poems
        to the lost brothers
        and sisters
        we loved too much.

When the poem vanishes
        —and it will from time-to-time—
        we will call it back
        by breathing in
        the color of the sky.

10 December 2019
La Cieneguilla; Santa Fe, New Mexico

Honey At The Check-Out Counter

Vivian has her name
      on a small paper badge
      clipped just below her blouse collar.

Vivian is the check-out lady
      in aisle 3 at Sprouts.

She knows the cost
      of bananas, blueberries and
      half-and-half
      without looking at the chart
      by the cash register.

Vivian speaks to those of us
      who line up,
      six-feet-apart,
      with metal carts
      of vegetables and fruit,
      juices and items
      from the bulk section of the store.

Vivian calls me Honey.

She may have called the man
      before me Honey too,
      but I don't mind.

Vivian's Honey is the sweetest
      on a late afternoon
      when the red pick-up truck
      rushed at me
      and newspaper headlines

call the American politicians
unreliable, dishonest and
untrustworthy.

Vivian's Honey gives me
the feeling I am reliable, honest
and trustworthy.

Vivian loves me and I love her.

18 February 2020
La Cieneguilla; Santa Fe, New Mexico
Published in *Iconoclast #122*, Mohegan Lake, NY 2021.

THIS IS WHERE I WELCOME YOU

Here,
    where summer dust devils
    chase leaves
    across a cattle guard,
    I stand with fence posts
    and barbed wire.

Here,
    I dream of September pears,
    where winter footprints of coyotes
    and foxes spring open in April,
    initiating flaming penstemon.

Here,
    when the moon is full,
    locust trees hold owls in their arms
    that field mice sing lullabies to.

Here is peace,
    where my shadow
    takes the shape
    of who loves me.

This is where I live.

This is where I welcome you.

12 November 2019
La Cieneguilla; Santa Fe, New Mexico

To Praise

Look into a mirror of water.

See your beginning,
        the flutter of feathers
        in your hair,
        the wild animal glare
        in your eyes,
        how your mouth opens
        and closes as the anemone
        in the tide pool.

        Praise.

Walk into the grasses of the earth,
        find a path of rabbit light
        hidden in buffalo burr and grama grass.
        You have walked here before
        in other lands.

        Praise.

Touch the home bark of tree,
        rub the oils from your skin
        into the wood. It has been waiting
        for your moisture.

        Praise.

Small the scent of growing things,
        blossoms,
        open green leaves,
        take a deep breath here,

breathe the in-and-out
of your original breath.

Praise.

Listen to bird song,
and below-earth song,
this is the chorus
that taught you
how to listen,
how to speak,
taught you what words to say
to shadows and sunlight.

Praise.

26 May 2020
La Cieneguilla; Santa Fe, New Mexico

via telephone with Cynthia West

A painted apple cannot be eaten.

Her photograph cannot see the moon
        or hear the stars falling,
        leaving holes as gates to heaven.

If I leave a stuffed, cotton mouse
        on the floor, Cat will believe
        it to be an offering for her
        to purr the shadows away.

The man down the road,
        buried his dog, Negro,
        last week. His sadness
        has kept his gate closed.

There is ice on the river now;
        cold silver clouds of frozen dreams.

When the sun steps through the gate
        of the mountain into the valley here,
        the river giggles and ripples
        into a canyon where cattails
        sleep in their Winter fluff.

A painted apple cannot be eaten.

Its seeds cannot be planted.

Should I hang its bright, round face
        above my bed, the red of its wildfire
        will keep me awake.

I shall leave a basket of apples
	at the gate of my neighbor
	in the afternoon sun.

14 December 2020
La Cieneguilla; Santa Fe, New Mexico

Things No One Can See

ONE

Tomorrow will be the memory
        and the not remembered.

If I forget you,
        it is only temporary.

You may return as a postage stamp,
        or the curve of a falling leaf.

If I step on your shadow, forgive me,
        I was looking at yesterday.

TWO

The afternoon sky has the appearance
        of being tired:
        holding up the refugees of clouds,
        feeling the sun and the wind
        breathing in-and-out,
        keeping space for flocks of jays
        and robins.

The sky shares its endless conversation
        with stones, mountains and rivers.

Lakes hold the sky of day in their palms
        until the moon drops its eye
        into the silence.

THREE

As the shadows of light criss-and-cross
        the wall, opposite where I sit,
        waterfalls appear, bits-and-pieces
        of ghosts, maps without destinations,
        faces that vanish before they smile or weep.

This is how time passes, changing like sand
        running through fingers.

        FOUR

Looking out the window, opposite where I sit,
        seeing branches of trees story-telling,
        a flock of birds worshipping the valley,
        a whisper of dust on the road,
        the wind is there,
        no sound comes through the window:
        I spread loneliness across the valley.

        FIVE

What brings the cat to jump into my lap
        when I read a poem?
        She is all fur-fire,
        orange and black,
        feet of winter wheat.

She lies down, facing that place
        where I see only a pillow
        and a lamp.

The poem read. The touch of fire.
    My pen tells her jumping,
    staring story.

        SIX

I must speak of death now
    because I may not see dandelions again
    or count the number of stars
    in Orion's Belt.

This does not mean fog or drought.

This does not mean loss of memory
    a touch of virus.

This means I only want you
    to sit and listen, to breathe.

        SEVEN

Yes. There are many kinds of breathing:
    the in-and-the-out,
    the morning freshness,
    the night of goodbye.

Breathing is invisible, except
    when your winter-breath
    clouds to moisten the glass
    in the door so I can write
    your name before the world vanishes.

        EIGHT

And if death comes unprepared for an embrace,
    I will ask it to wait its turn,
    I have deer to count and apples to pick.

I will offer it a chair and a glass of water
    from the well.

1 December 2020
La Cieneguilla; Santa Fe, New Mexico

via telephone with Cynthia West
Published in *The Deronda Review Vol IX, No 1*, Efrat, Israel.

The Poet's House

Chile has Neruda.

France has Baudelaire.

England has Blake.

Japan has Basho.

China has Li Po.

Galisteo has Ferguson.
Cerro Gordo has West.

In their houses
        are journals,
        cups of broken pencils,
        scattered papers,
        pillows that talk all night
        and rugs that whisper sonnets
        about dust and the voices
        of mysterious footsteps.

A house is their temple,
        their altar,
        their light,
        the candle that burns their eyes,
        ink in their pens for blood transfusions.

Here are tea bags
        and coffee strainers,
        dogs and cats
        with poems lining their litter boxes.

Trails of bread crumbs
        walk from their doors
        to the river bank
        and into the mountain
        where stones are asking
        for the word love
        to be etched on their faces
        that stare at sunburned clouds.

All this is the poet's house,
        river,
        mountain,
        stone,
        words dropped
        after the bread crumbs
        have been eaten by crows.

Here are walls of coyote wails,
        roofs of deer tracks,
        floors of apple peelings.

This is the dwelling of solitude,
        even when the trees
        outside my window
        wave at me.

30 January 2021
La Cieneguilla; Santa Fe, New Mexico

I Am Home Now

I am home now.

On days the gophers and I
        go underground,
        we eat our roots,
        leaving ancestors to their silence.

On days the sparrows and I
        crack sunflower seeds,
        we share unsprouted nourishment.

The windows need washing.

The floors need mopping.

Hinges on the doors need oiling.

I will keep the shadows
        that follow me
        outside
        in the woodpile.

Old shadows are pitch-filled
        for the kitchen fireplace.

This could be a roaring fire
        of patriotic march music
        and hymns of grief,
        to match the bubbling
        of wild rose-hip jam
        and mint jelly.

There never is a lock
        on the back door.

Neighbors might get slivers
        from the wood
        if they enter
        without knocking.

Locust trees
        around the house
        are older now,
        taller.

They continue
        to reach
        toward the clouds.

The heart carved
        on the pear tree is faded:
        names there are unreadable.

Who was it who loved me?

4 February 2021
La Cieneguilla; Santa Fe, New Mexico

A Warrior-Poet Comes Home

It was twenty years of found-and-lost,
        of combat-and-peace.

Today,
        I send my poems flying
        to the beloveds who kept me singing.

I left TADAO behind in Misawa:

        my love poems
        come to you
        as cherry blossoms falling in Ueno

I left YEIKO in Okinawa:

        we will hear
        each other singing
        in the hibiscus

I left KIM, YOUNG HAE in Seoul:

        let us write
        the names of birds
        we hear
        hidden in the clouds
        of Bon Won Sa
        to remember our names

I left KLAUDIA in Frankfurt:

        there are
        only songbirds
        in the Schwarzwald

I left NADIM in Kabul:

> *we lost time*
> *we lost one another*
> *before we started*
> *did you know*
> *it was too early*
> *to pick pomegranates*

I left LEYLA in Baghdad:

> *your death*
> *and mine*
> *are but falling feathers*

Today,
>   I sit in my orchard, where everything is secret,
>   listening to birds singing:

> *I shall return to you*
> *each night*
> *the moon returns*
> *to the mountain*

I listen but hear only echoes.

10 January 2021
La Cieneguilla; Santa Fe, New Mexico

Ghosts

The ghosts in my room
      are honey colored and soft to touch.

They lie in corners and under cupboards.

They collect mouse fluff for blankets.

They nibble at the edges of pine logs
      for the fire place.

They rub ashes in their hair
      so we cannot see them.

The ghosts in my room
      have ancient ears filled with myth
      and mystery.

They have woven the stories
      of many years into the walls
      of my room, hung their favorite
      words of love and anger on nails
      hidden behind paintings
      and treasured objects.

When I am quiet, open, receptive
      they hold my hands,
      move my pen across the paper
      to become the spirits
      who speak for me.

The ghosts in my room
      wear my clothes, breathe my breath,
      they call me by my name.

2 March 2018
Galisteo, New Mexico

ABOUT THE POET

Poet, James McGrath, offers *A Temporary Silence* as his eighth book with Sunstone Press of Santa Fe, New Mexico, USA.

James lives in La Cieneguilla Village near Santa Fe, New Mexico. He is noted for his narrative poetry in the PBS/KAET American Indian Artists Series in the 1970s. In 2008, he was designated a Santa Fe Living Treasure. The Institute of American Indian Arts awarded James their Visionary Award in 2010. In 2014, he was given the Gratitude Award by New Mexico Literary Arts for his contribution to the literary life of New Mexico. In 2015, the University of Baltimore's *passager*'s editors awarded him their 2015 Poet Award. *The Kerf* of the College of the Redwoods in Crescent City, California in 2019, nominated his poem, "Drawing Pictures," for a Pushcart Prize. James was United States Information Service, Arts America, poet/artist in residence in Yemen, the Kingdom of Saudi Arabia and the Republic of the Congo in the 1990s. A biography of James, *James McGrath: In A Class By Himself*, by Jonah Raskin, author of *American Scream: Allen Ginsberg's "Howl" and the Making of the Beat Generation*, was published in 2012.

SELF PORTRAIT IN THE TIME OF VIRUS

When I write my self portrait poem,
    I will not look into any aging mirror.

I will not reread my crumpled letters
    to Mom and Dad from childhood.

Instead, I will walk my dirt road
    after a rain, look into the murky pools
    of water to read my wrinkled face.

It is woven of reflected decisions
    that fill my path with fertile adventures.

My face will be the home
    where I took off the mask
    when you kissed away the emptiness
    from my journey.

This is the self portrait I write
    on my ceiling with words of praise
    when I open my eyes at the morning gate
    to find your shadow lying next to me.